*for my friend &
favorite bee keeper - max*

♡ Chelsea

deer | woman

poems by

Chelsea DuVall

Finishing Line Press
Georgetown, Kentucky

deer | woman

Copyright © 2018 by Chelsea DuVall
ISBN 978-1-63534-524-7 First Edition
All rights reserved under International and Pan-American Copyright Conventions. No part of this book may be reproduced in any manner whatsoever without written permission from the publisher, except in the case of brief quotations embodied in critical articles and reviews.

acknowledgements

It started with Douglas Kearney and Alice Tuan; these beloved artists and mentors encouraged me to pick up the pen, and supported my early explorations in creative writing (playwriting, specifically). Without them, this work would not be before you. Other glorious contributors include; Kjartan Ingvarsson, Addison Hart, Guillermo Maytorena and Travis Wagoner (cover art). To these talented and beautiful people, in addition to the loved ones who offer continual support to me in my artistic endeavors—you have my gratitude.

"d e e r | w o m a n" appeared in *STARK, The Poetry Journal*, edited by Jeanette Skirvan & Sam Vaseghi, No 2, l'Aleph, 2017, p. 67.

Publisher: Leah Maines
Editor: Christen Kincaid
Cover Art and Design: Travis Wagoner
Author Photo: Julia Marcus

Printed in the USA on acid-free paper.
Order online: www.finishinglinepress.com
   also available on amazon.com

Author inquiries and mail orders:
Finishing Line Press
P. O. Box 1626
Georgetown, Kentucky 40324
U. S. A.

Table of Contents

fog

d e e r | w o m a n

'til now

Two women

a Francesca

b Francesca

presume, assume, the anti-bloom

Fool me

h i d e & s e e k

Thoughts

She stands

The lights of Georgia

the piano

Steeping

Awakening

A match

Catch

Collateral light

soft sheets

e x X

The tide of a torso

Snow falling on headstones

Time, as it moves

introduction

It's strange, but true; in my dreams, my family is still together, still unhappy. History unravels itself in these little fantasies, returning all the figures and pieces to a familiar checkpoint, a place of normalcy—if not necessarily of satisfaction. Everything that has followed along in waking life, even to a degree the structure of my own personality, is now allowed to recede harmlessly to the furthest point of the dream. I am free to imagine another life—another self.

In introducing this little book of poetry, memories of these dreams creep through my mind. Inevitably, I suppose, as Chelsea and I have such similar experiences of early life. The points of comparison are numerous and obvious. We are both the eldest of two children, our parents are divorced, our fathers were clergymen, our mothers suffer from precisely the same psychological disease. Clergy can travel about a great deal; even in periods of stability, we were used to adapting ourselves to new environments quickly, learning not to grow overly attached to the scenery. Both of us would become inveterate ramblers in our own right, never living in any one spot long enough to acquire any truly continuous sense of place. When I look at a map of the United States, I see fragments of myself almost everywhere. I can't simply go sweep them up; some are people, constantly moving about themselves, and some are houses, inaccessible to me. I have dreams of them as well, all my old family homes, which I find myself continually emptying of their contents—perhaps out of some real duty to remove them, or else because I can't quite conceive of how to break free of my need for them. Certain objects would follow me to every new location; they provided a link, served as a kind of memorial chain. Without them, I am forced to rely on my imagination.

It doesn't surprise me to find that Chelsea's own imaginative life contains such a deep impression of fragmentation, of the need to reassemble and obtain a sense of belonging. Fantasy, for us, is very much a question of our surroundings. In dreams, in fiction, in poetry, the same theme continually arises: that intense longing, not necessarily for any one place, but for a substitute to every place.

When our friendship began, our surroundings were very inauspicious indeed. We were students at an obscure college in a small town 'in the heart of the heart of the country'—which is to say, on a plain as flat and nondescript as the Tartar Steppe, populated mostly by cornstalks and pigs, and designed (where such a word may be applied) along monotonous patterns of unbending lines. It was, moreover, generally lacking in bookshops, cinemas, restaurants, landscapes, and even shadows. A wan, urine-yellow sunlight pervaded at all hours of the day and in every corner, transforming nature into a thin tan paste and keeping one continually bobbing along in a state of nauseated somnambulance. Kant, presumably, would have referred to this realm as a 'far-reaching solitude'; I considered it a bore myself, alleviated only by certain friendships made there.

The earliest distinct memory I have of Chelsea is of hearing her shout my name across a considerable distance as I negotiated the maze of identical buildings comprising the campus. I halted in my tracks as she swiftly overtook me. I knew I recognized her, and that she recognized me was patently obvious, but it took more than a moment to place her. I had, as it turned out, a history of shrieking into her ear myself, though for a quite respectable reason, and on occasion melodiously too, as I stood behind her in the bass section of a choir. (It's clear, in retrospect, why I hadn't remembered this at once. Like so many aspects of life in that town, the choir simply faded from my mind when I wasn't there, slipping away at precisely the moment I left the room and returning to me only at the instant of my reappearance one week later, as if some occult mechanical process had guided me back.) But it didn't matter whether I remembered her or not; she chatted to me as though she had known me all her life; in this way, our friendship seemed always to have been. Charmed, I took the precaution of memorizing her name—but there was little need to take such a tremendous effort, as she was soon besieging me with invitations and observations and opportunities to step out of the little nest I'd made to escape the dreariness of the place. She seemed to stand apart in every way from her surroundings. I enjoyed her intelligence and good humor, her elfin sort of beauty, her curiosity, even her alarming tendency to nibble on the strands of her raven-black hair. She was, crucially, alive, where so little else appeared to be. And it became obvious, after only a few conversations (we are both very frank and exceedingly garrulous), that we had a great deal in common, and saw the world in similar terms. From this root sprung a friendship that was, for me, refreshing, exciting, strange at times, comforting, always delightful (the reader may continue to imagine a list of superlatives at her leisure).

As we came to the end of our time in that place, we saw less and less of one another. She had entered into a serious relationship, the trajectory of which may be discerned from the poems in this collection. Moreover, she was considerably more attentive to her work than I was to mine, and consequently busier as a rule. Still, we exchanged books from time to time, went on walks, had our occasional lunches together, and parted warmly as she left to find work on the other side of the country. Over the half decade or so that has since elapsed, we have maintained a steady correspondence, and so, at a remove, I have continued to watch her experience certain of the joys and shocks of her life, and observe to a limited degree her development as an artist—as actor, singer, dramatist, and even now as the author of this book. All the while, she has continued to move about, circumstances have continued to change.

In the poems in the present collection, only one state remains constant; there is only one continuous space, and that is the body itself. Everywhere the reader is presented with a holistic sense of the poet. Sinews echo with the sounds of their own operation, joints ache, faces rest placidly over skulls. It is not merely a question of mechanisms. Whispers arise from 'a cavity of marrow', as in ancient times spirits issued from certain fissures in the earth. These mysterious portals— omphaloi to the Greeks, mundi to the Romans—were quite literally understood as navels by which the region of the living was joined to the underworld. From these points of connection, invisible cords traveled from the terrestrial domain down into an unknown place, a realm of origination subtly mirroring what lay above and implying in this sympathy an obscure possibility of completeness in the liminal space between the two. We hear the quiet echo of this mythology in Chelsea's poetry, where human bodies are found to possess their own complex geographies. Of hers we are granted an exclusive cartographical vision; she guides us into the subterranean narrows of her own blood and bone, each of her poems acting as a compass rose. In this place of underworld fumes, we breathe the spiritual essence of the poet's voice. Chelsea thus writes from the perspective of her own soul, speaking out of its primordial home.

In her verses, no concern is greater than the longing for completeness—a longing we hear ourselves echo. The poems sway, as August Schlegel wrote generally of modern verse, 'between memory and anticipation'—memory of a lost world, anticipation of another to be found. The discrete objects of our desire will vary, from the bliss of erotic love, a sympathetic god, satisfaction or closure in a relationship, or a return to some blissful and uncomplicated state, but the original underlying impression remains, compelling all these needs. It is the conviction that we are dislocated beings, mysterious exiles from the world. In our apprehension of this exile, a void of uncertain dimensions is formed. We fill it with what we can—memories; daydreams; idle observations of the passage of clouds; the savor of briefly suspended moments of calm and pleasure; certain fragrances, colors; sometimes with the perpetuation of desire itself; the sight of green hillsides in the mineral sweetness of rain; books of poetry; with luck, the surprise of love.

—Addison Hart

fog

She sensed something strange was approaching.
We should run a little further,
she said to her wounded wrists.

deer | woman

Her body would not lie to you.

You see not the truth before you,
her whispering certainty
        residing in a cavity of marrow.

Her tempo answers to the breeze;
fast in fear,
slow in caution.

Her body is her own;
at once in softness,
at once in strength.

It is only when the orbs align
that her spirit flashes before you;
permission,
fear and stillness
        captured within her azure eyes.

She stands the fawn;
between grace
        and gravity.
She stands the doe;
between the wild
        and warped worlds.
She stands the stag;
between vitality,
power
        and hunted fragility.

She stands before you.

Some will set their eyes to her,
some will follow her through the wildwood;
        a labyrinth of flora and fauna,
some desire to wipe her memory from forest green.

Between fantasy
        and folklore,
                between dreams
                          and myth,
she stands before you.

'til now

I have never lived 'til now.

'til these fibers raise to heaven,
pulling skin from bone.
'til sweat pours from every pore,
swelling in a shallow tide upon the smooth wood.
I have never lived
       'til this heat erupts with violent will,
this current arching my spine,
stretching this body along plush planes.

'til this force overtakes me,
'til this yearning overwhelms,
'til this voice escapes these lungs,
'til these limbs ignite,
'til these fingers dig deeper,
'til this focus is sharpened,
'til the cool numb darkness
       explodes into hot, white light.

No, not once have I lived.

Two women

I am one woman
                              and the other

two spines coiling into another,
twisting,
        traipsing
                            and twirling,

oily droplets draping the discs

I am one woman
                              and the other
laughing and crying
        to myself,

neurons fighting nature,
        cells fighting
                            other cells

I am one strand of hair,
        hanging in these eyes
        blurring the version
                            on either side

If I look in the mirror
        am I one woman
                            or the other

If you look at me
        am I one woman
                            or the other

Am I myself
                            or yours

a Francesca

I relinquish this body to the builder;
    I collapse, I concede
    I submit, I surrender

If I stay here a little longer,
    it will get easier,
    I will get tired and forget

b Francesca

The words slid down the soft surface of my arms, poured into my joints;
    they went directly to my hands.
They passed through my hands along the painted surface;
    they floated over layers of color.
They expanded to the corners of the room and ran along the floorboards.
They cut through dust, chalk and broken glass;
    they rippled through the solid surface of earth.
They climbed high, reaching for the ceiling;
    they travelled far above my body.
They move at the speed of light, dancing faster than the eye can trace.
They raced towards the door, the brass knob just out of reach.
They danced towards the cool breeze of the open window;
    they dream of barren sky.

presume, assume, the anti-bloom

I do not presume you to know my soul.
    To understand how far this cave travels below,
    to pitch a soft light in the deafening darkness.

No, I would not presume so much.
    I do not presume you to know my mind,
    how quickly it spins and toils fibers of thought into twine.

I do not presume, do not assume
    anything so heavy as that upon my shoulders,
    here within the echoes of my chamber.

No, I do not.

But desire outweighs presumption.
    desire overshadows logic
    and tears at the sinew of reality;
    (desire) she is a haunted and deadly mistress.

I do not presume I shall let her in,
    though she knows my every sin.

She knocks,
she knocks,
she stands too near.
    she whispers seductively into my ear.

I do not presume I can defeat her,
    I cannot be so naive.

But should she swallow my soul,
    even that she will never know.

Fool me

Again and again
I sin and I sin.
Living and loving,
and hardly recovering.
Again and again,
Betrayed by my skin.
I drown and I die,
My sinew screams, sharp and dry.
I fall and I fail,
And in failure I flail,
removing the top skin
weightless and thin.
This string pulls hard.
This tiny glass shard
it burns and it chokes,
I'm smothered in smoke.
I paint myself black,
I lie on my back,
repeating the verse
and reliving the curse.

hide & seek

My mother hides in a dark room at the end of a long hall

She hides behind a walnut door with a golden brass knob
    under manufactured sheets and soft down
        the horizontal blinds pulled tight telling the daylight to keep away
        the only light from a small television
            her dark marbles illuminated and captured by the cool glow
            her eyes are open but she's sleeping
            her eyes are open but she's shut
like the walnut door with the golden brass knob

She hides in this room with necklaces draped about the walls
    and closets crammed full of clothing
        clothing hiding bodies
            she's buried beneath beads boxes and bottles
            always in excess

She's hiding in Mary's medicine cabinet
    while I converse with ivory
    and dance with a soft white kitten

She hides from little feet pattering down the hall
    and apple trees in the backyard
    behind soup bowls
        spoonful after spoonful
        she hides as her daughter feeds her
        her eyes do not look up
        not once

She hides in rehabilitation centers counseling meetings and group sessions
    and still she hides behind dark walls
    and tiny television sets daytime T.V.
    sterling silver vanilla mascara curling irons aerosols
    caravans and pill bottles
    always in excess

She hides
        from her children
        from her husband and his congregation
        past present and future
        from the frame that contains her spirit
        she's hiding from herself

We would seek her
> run after her but she's too far away
> too far to the Borderline
> our tiny legs are not strong enough
>> to fight against the mountains of sinking sand
>> and stranded empty bottles
> we would run after her
>> but all we know is the blue in our eyes
>> and the scent of vanilla

So we wait
> because we only believe this to be a storm
> a passing pattern
>> The thing about patterns
>> ...
>> ...
>> ...
>> they return
>> (fools)

We wait
> over the mountains into the swamplands and returning to the evergreen

We wait through
> boyfriends dirty cigarettes run away marriages
> orange juice that's not orange juice
>> (it looked like orange juice)
> dance clubs and loud music
> screaming fighting gnashing of rotten teeth
> long fingernails scraping the sidewalk

we wait
> for phone calls and rides home
> we play video games make mix tapes
> to drown out the screaming and coughing

We wait
> for years
> some of us are still waiting
>> still dreaming
>>> to see the glimmer of her blue marble
>> still dreaming
>>> that she pulls the sheets from her body
>>> swings her legs over the side of the bed
>>> and walks strongly along the paved path
>> still dreaming

that her teeth are no longer falling out

some of us try
some of us grow tired of waiting
some of us give up
some of us recognize the pattern
    and it grows like a dark seed inside us

no more
this game isn't fun

(it never was fun to begin with)

you are left seeking
or waiting alone
in the dark

Thoughts

But I have so many,
she thought.
Turning 'round within my cap;
a Ferris-wheel of fire.

She stands

She stands,
palms kissing the surface of the wind.

She stands,
head tilted under a canopy of stars.

She stands,
wisps of fine hair trailing behind her curved spine.

She stands,
waiting, waiting, waiting
       for someone to come blow her away.

The lights of Georgia

How do you reconcile this?
This pain.
This ever-present, numbing pulse
        which beats against the skin of my humanity,
        which humiliates my pride.
How do you navigate?
These waters
        tainted tides of the polluted past
        which flood the tissue of my frail lungs.
How do you resist?
This urge,
        this aching desire to pound out the misery
        trapped within the cracked caverns of this cranium.
...
...
...
How do you not take your fist full of diamonds,
        and shove them so far down the well
        that the lights go out in Georgia?

the piano

She couldn't tell you how it came to be that the ash was scattered about the house, couldn't tell you how a thin layer of soot blanketed every surface. Or how the windows leaked light through jagged cracks and fragmented shards. Or how the walls curled into the center of the room. How the floorboards shifted below footsteps. She couldn't tell you how everything became a spoiled version of an ideal, slowly turning to rotten fruit.

But there, she sat.

Familiar figures floated about her, familiar and estranged. They pressed upon her body, manipulating the space between her limbs. She knew the voices, could trace a faint scent as they passed. There was a vague recognition in the fine distinctions of their features. They were known to her. She knew them by name, as the branch upon a tree. But they remained strangers. They pressed and pushed and shuffled her as cards on the table. They pressed upon her but remained just… beyond… her… reach, beyond affection and comfort. They moved themselves away from her as quickly as they rushed toward her; there, and gone. But mostly, gone. They moved themselves away from her because they moved themselves further from themselves, retreating to shadow. They could not look at her because they could not look at themselves.

And there, she sat.

She sat with her companion of smooth auburn planks, which mirrored the glow of her fine hair. Together, they were copper, fire and warm afternoon sun. Together they existed in slivers of sunlight in the dust filled oikos. She sat, reaching for the only embrace that would receive her, the only voice that would return the call. Their connection dispelled the shadows with every strike, lighting the dark corners with a burst of flame. Her slender fingers would never forget the smooth surface, the gentle receptacle that awaited her touch, and cradled her identity. She always thought her fingers had too many knobs, protruding like a virus from the trunk of a tree.

She sees them and remembers her father.

But as she placed them back upon the shelled surface, they stretched and thinned, and danced on shining wood like a figure on ice. The slender digits manifest the senses, guiding her through the memories of a melody, or clumsily attempting to construct a new fantasy.

Just there, she sat.

This beautiful instrument would extend her call across the ruined history and pained present.

"I will be heard," she thought.

It was for herself that she played. And sometimes, for him, the dark-haired man wrestling with reality, wrestling to change the reality before him. He painted their house with a brush all too hopeful and diluted with delusional optimism. Wrestling, painting, baking fresh batches of cookies into the night, and slowly gagging himself with the strings of his grey apron. He was everywhere else, and then in the kitchen—this is where she could reach him.

She played, she sat.

She could never see him, only feel his presence from beyond the dividing wall. Nor could she hear his step as he entered the archway, or smell the crisp bacon on the hot stove. She could not see him, but the music found its way past the curling walls to the center of his curled character.

She started to play, softly at first, allowing the melody to carve a pathway through the dusted air, searching for the listener. Each note struck the air with a desperate beauty, blurring the pointed blue of her eyes. She grew. The hammers violently struck of a determined hope, which would remain only that. The expression expanded, pounding the ruined walls, swelling to a steady shake. The structure was crumbling, though remaining in ruin. She played, pounding on pedals and kicking the keys, vibrating the delicate skeleton of a family that would remain under the ashes.

Only he was listening,
      but somehow
           missed her song.

It's a tree.

                              It's an ocean.

It's a tree.

                              It's an ocean.

It's a tree.

                              It's an ocean.

She played,
      she stopped.
She stopped,
      she cried.

And there, she sat.
      Alone, as she once was.

The song was lost. The momentum dismembered from her desire. Even if the soles of her skeleton dug in the pedals, nothing could transcend the moment the music would cease, the moment she stopped, and returned to the solitude of her freckled frame.

      Nothing would remain.

Steeping

Only tea leaves circling the vessel.

And a gaze,
a gentle blue breeze
washing stillness over this feeble frame.

There is nothing before you
        but the woman waiting within.

Awakening

She remembers laying back into the clouds,
and sinking deep into the silent sounds of their embrace.

She remembers his kindly kisses,
and the tame tenderness of his touch.

She remembers pushing back the sun from his eyes,
and feeling the cool, blue sea.

She remembers the insistent, incessant pulsing of his moans,
and the sliding of the chords as she spoke the words of his body.

She remembers the rhythm of his pleasure, a careful waltz,
the throbbing tempo knocking at her door.

She remembers the warmth of his beating body,
the sweet sensation of sweat and satisfaction.

She remembers that he left her,
just as the flames were rising...

What, said she,
        shall I do with this awakening?

A match

Sometimes the torch turns on the village, and itself.
Sometimes the fire believes it is only a spark,
or the light leading the way.
Sometimes the roaring waters believe they are birthing the truth
       instead of drowning the masses.
Sometimes you paint the stone black,
douse it in gasoline and strike a match.
You burn the forest again and again and again.
And water the smoking haystack.

Catch

We throw a ball to one another;

    yours
            mine
                  yours
                        mine
                              yours

Sailing over the green grass from my hand to yours,

        mine
                yours

The sound of the snap never sounded so sweet as it does in that moment,

    mine

And you remind me—snap.
"I still have it,"

    yours
        mine

No matter how long it's been, my palm always remembers the slight sting ... it numbs after awhile,

    yours

We don't talk,
don't need to talk,
just send this sphere high into the air.
It's the clearest language we speak.

We don't talk of crosses or pentagrams,
of ashes and the body of Christ
"It really does work, " you say,
you talk of prayer, and I listen.

We don't talk of arrows,
broken and unbroken.
Of rainbows behind wooden doors,
and the secret married life of strangers.

We don't talk of damaged hallways, or spots on dishes.
We don't talk about long drives with hammers in the trunk.
We don't talk about institutional intervention,
tears and judgement.

We don't talk ... just toss a ball into the atmosphere.

Collateral light

You lie asleep
under a night of frosted stars.
Holding tight something
that was already yours.

I lie here
searching in the darkness
for my dignity.

It travels up.
A mad heat rushing up my arms,
tendrils of terror.

You sleep in a canopy of comfort and pleasure.
Your limbs locked
with fair skin,
just to your liking.

I feel the wind escape from my gut.
It takes my breath away
and wrings dry tears from my soft skull.

I shake the image,
I slam the set,
the picture fades,
but the hurt,
        it hums.

soft sheets

I place myself there
        just there
        on the corner of the bed
        one foot rests upon the sea
        the other on the wood.

I place you there
        on the same corner
        staring back at me
        to see myself.

I paint white lace gloves
        on your fingers
        rubbing the inside of your knees.

I see the reluctant sinew
        staring back at me
        searching for yourself.

On the corner of the bed we sit
        gazing into ourselves
        and into the eyes of the other.

We
        a clouded mirror of the other form.

Soft light
soft sheets
dark bodies.

There you sit
        and this would be mine.

Yes
        this still would be mine.

e x X

You think because I'm locked in the closet that I won't kick any harder.
That I won't set the house on fire,
air your dirty laundry
and smash plates against the garage door.

That I won't tear at labels
and shatter pill bottles.
Do you think I'm so simple?
So docile and subservient.

You think you can bite me,
hold me under and batter me with bruises.
You wrangled the wrong woman.
You aren't so bright to underestimate.
Your teeth marks were smarter than you,
and more attractive.

Early on, I saw.
The passenger window of your Ford never looked so clear
as we drove home from mirrored infinity.
A single red flag,
bright as daylight.
Red.
A warning lingering on your breath,
on a single phrase.
My thoughts turned for a moment,
I reasoned, I compromised.

All became clear as we slept side by side,
as you tried to coax your cock down my throat.
I still wish I would have left bite marks,
as dark as the purple which decorated my limbs.
Spending nights beneath hanging wardrobe,
trying not to smell your feet.
Making friends with the linoleum
and flushing your diagnosis.

You tried
to erase my ambition.
You tried, but…
I would choose a dull book to your short stack,
a cold tile floor to your clammy hands,
and the rug burning bruises to donning iron aprons.

I surprised you, didn't I?
Left you astonished and shocked.
You didn't see the fire within,
the dragon inside the damsel,
because you never saw me.
You were too busy looking at your own reflection
in the irises of my eyes.

Taste the fire on my breath
and the water of my womb.
I don't think you were alive before you met me.

Go find your picket fence.
Go strangle another woman,
pump her full of your liquid cowardice.
Tie a collar 'round her neck,
and drag her down the street.
Go find another wench to rub your feet
and place a pillow beneath your head.
Go find an empty vessel without a life,
without dreams or aspirations.
Go find a lady to get in bed with your family,
to suck your fainting phallus,
and swallow little blue pills.
Go find yourself a servant,
because you do not want a woman.

You can change the locks
and sign the papers,
but you will still have to answer for your fists,
your teeth and your cock.

You will always be a monster in my memory,
a baby sucking on his mother's teat.
You wrangled the wrong woman.
You laid a hand on the wrong warrior.

I'm glad it's not my job to punish or scold,
I hope your shame and ego never let you forget
my smiling face as I signed on the dotted line.

No regrets.
The day you divorced the dragon
and I the blubbering adolescent.

The tide of a torso

I met a tall man with the ocean in his eyes,
        and the sandy shore in his tussled locks.
A man whose soft voice and gentle touch
        persuaded the fire under my skin to follow him home.
He pulled carefully close and blew his baled breath on the breach of my back.
We walked along the edge of the earth,
        among rust-colored beasts.
I looked up at him and saw the sun.
I looked out to the green, graceful grasses of the Garden
        and easily accepted the soft surface of simplicity.

He sang poetry not his own, and completely his own. His placid pipes offering quiet, intimate artistry. I watched his fingers dance across the vibrating vessel, and I smiled.

I met a tall man and tried to steal away in the night,
        leaving him to tow the tide.
He grabbed my hand
        and asked me to stay.
His warmth enveloped this effete embodiment,
        shaking and swollen with sadness.

I met a tall man with the ocean in his eyes
        and an anchor for his heart.
I watched as he unfurled his pain
        and allowed his tall frame to bend into the comfort of my paltry palms.
His torso trembled, growing cathartic
        and calm beside this melancholy maiden.

There, beside him,
        in the despondent darkness,
        we made light of our own.

I followed the light through narrow hallways and cold corridors.
I followed it to London and back again.

I followed it into noisy pubs, tethered tents
        and over the crowded cobblestone.

I followed the light as it seeped from his sideways smile
        and struggled with sly sentiment.

I followed the light too far,
    I reached too far beyond the limits of this lithe body.

I followed it across the ocean
    and into the terror of transition.
It grew dainty and dim,
    frail and fragile.
I tried to preserve it,
    save it.
I tried to shield it,
    to shelter it.

And in the struggle,
    I strangled the supple splendor.

We were without light.

I met a tall man with the ocean in his eyes,
    and without looking,
        plunged into the dark depths.

Snow falling on headstones

I see you in the cemetery.
Walking on the frost-bitten flora,
your dark hair burns against a sheet of white.
The ground is soft and hard beneath our souls,
frozen petals shattering like bones.

Colored glass startles the stone walls,
as the snow bleeds into your pale skin.
There a moment, and gone,
changing before my gaze.
My breath meets you before the words.

I see you in the cemetery
walking in a flood of distant carols.
Walking towards one another
and miles apart.

Would she cross the ocean to walk upon the bones?
To see her breath linger in a cemetery,
beside the one with whom she shall rest.

Time, as it moves

She saw everything and nothing.
She felt the current of her breath traversing her tissue.
She counted the possibilities on his skin,
and decided not to turn back.

Chelsea **DuVall** is an international theatre artist and writer. She completed her Masters of Fine Arts in Acting, with supplemental studies in Playwriting, at the California Institute of the Arts (2015), and her Bachelors of Arts in Theatre Studies at Northern Illinois University (2010). Her poetry has appeared in *STARK*, and her completed theatrical works include; *Francesca, Francesca…, (anti)Matter* and *Sonic Insurgency*. Her plays have been produced by the following; On The Boards Open Studio (Seattle, WA), 2015 Edinburgh Fringe Festival, The California Institute of the Arts and The Pocket Theater (Seattle, WA).

CPSIA information can be obtained
at www.ICGtesting.com
Printed in the USA
LVHW04s2057070618
580034LV00001B/35/P